Ideas on Wings

Ideas on Wings

A Collection of Poems
from the Christian Science Periodicals

The Christian Science Publishing Society
Boston, Massachusetts, U.S.A.

Edited by Carol Chapin Lindsey
Photographs by Gordon N. Converse
Design and Typography by Howard I. Gralla

ISBN 0-87510-120-8

Printed in the United States of America

Foreword

The thread that traces the history of man's worship of God is spun of many strands. One of the longest, perhaps the strongest, is poetry. The language in which men have spoken of God's presence and love, described His effect in the world, and encouraged each other to abide by His laws has often been a language beyond prose.

It has been a poetic language flowing from and leading into inspiration, whereby our ideals are minted into words that surprise us into fresh assessments of reality. It has been a language expressing not only reason but feeling. It has drawn to itself the many devices of metaphor, carrying one idea on the wings of another and saying many things in few words. Moreover, it has been a language attentive to the musicality of speech, in which words of all timbres lend their tones to the harmony of the whole. And it has been a language of rhythms, where the beat of sound on silence carves new channels in thought and opens the way to revelation.

Not surprisingly, the Bible abounds with poetry. As much as one third of the Old Testament, some scholars say, is in verse. These verse forms establish between writer and reader a set of shared expectations. Part of our pleasure as readers is in seeing just how the pattern of these expectations is to be fulfilled.

Beyond that, these forms help the writer by driving him to search for solutions, leading him to turns of phrase he might not otherwise have discovered. The good writer, if he is to fashion out of human speech a poetic voice charged with spiritual insight, needs several things. He must have something to say, a message in accord with his highest conception of Deity. To say it clearly, he needs to be skilled in his craft, having an eye for everything words do beyond their dictionary meanings. And he must somehow share, in ways that elude linguistic analysis, the fire of inspiration.

These essentials of message, skill, and inspiration were not foreign to Mary Baker Eddy.[1] No stranger to the poet's realm, she was a verse-maker from childhood.[2] She wrote a number of poems, seven of which have been set to music and are included in the *Christian Science Hymnal.* Not surprisingly, her regard for poetry carried over into the periodicals she founded. Several of her poems were first published there. Today *The Christian Science Journal,* the *Christian Science Sentinel, The Herald of Christian Science,* and *The Christian Science Monitor* regularly publish original poetry along with prose. And, except for those in the *Monitor,* all of the poems are directly related to the teachings of Christian Science and written by members of The Mother Church.

Each of the poems collected here first appeared in the pages of the *Sentinel* or the *Journal* during the past decade. On the basis of message, they are grouped into six sections. Those in the first section, "Direction," seek to articulate the relevance of Spirit to questions of aim and purposefulness. Further sections explore equally significant topics—the need for a sense of Christianity that brings genuine comfort, that explains individuality, that lifts thought to aspiration, and that embraces whatever breadth of experience humanity can envision. The final section focuses on the primitive, ongoing, and highly practical power of the Science of Christ in healing sickness, sin, and death.

In prosody and poetic strategy the poems are no less varied. They range in length from four to fifty-two lines, in design from hymnlike quatrains of perfect tetrameter to the freest of prose rhythms, in conception from insights into mortal illusions to statements of absolute Truth. They include such time-honored and exacting forms as the sonnet, the villanelle, and the ballade—the latter (see "Ballade for the Commandments," 7) requiring the poet to weave only three rhyme sounds through twenty-eight different rhyming words. They include a variety of parallel structures, as in the stanzas of "All-presence" (1) and the repeated lines of "Immutably Themselves" (21). They move from the relaxed conversational tone of such poems as "At This Very Hour, in This Very Place" (10) and "Radical Steps" (63) to the high formal mode of "The Shepherd Boy" (27) and "Pure Mind" (52). Some are timely, like "Zion-prayer" (54); some, like "Uncalendared" (58), are timeless. Some, like "Multitude-loving" (47), show us the thought freely musing over biblical history and contemporary relevance. Others, like "More Blessed" (45), pack biblical allusion, spiritual interpretation, and pithy insight into few words. Throughout, there are wonderful touches of musicality, as when, in "Summoned by Psaltery, Timbrel, and Harp" (12), the long *i*, short *a*, and *s* sounds intertwine to enliven the line "like the aftermath of a crisis passed," or when similar congregations of assonance and alliteration bind together these lines from "And in Their Mouths Is Found No Guile" (26):

> innocence fresher than first-of-morning light,
> sweeter than waters fountaining from a source
> high in bright hills.

Insofar as the poems gathered here really are inspired, they bear record—in different ways for different readers—to the power and understanding that regenerate and heal. They are not meant simply as decorations; if they are effective, they will help something good happen to the reader.

Rushworth M. Kidder

[1] Mary Baker Eddy is the Discoverer and Founder of Christian Science and author of *Science and Health with Key to the Scriptures*; [2] See *Retrospection and Introspection*, p. 11.

"Whether we build for centuries hence
or let tomorrow bound our aim,
God sets the pace."

Direction

1 All-presence

Peter J. Henniker-Heaton

We cannot turn away from God
because, whichever way we face,
Spirit is there. In every place,
every direction, everywhere,
Spirit is there.

Whether we turn to left or right,
to north or south or east or west,
we meet with Love—and we are blessed.
Upward or down, below, above,
we meet with Love.

Whether we plunge to ocean trench
or plot our course for farthest space,
Love's law controls. Whatever race
we enter toward whatever goals,
Love's law controls.

Whether we build for centuries hence
or let tomorrow bound our aim,
God sets the pace. Always the same,
with instant and eternal grace,
God sets the pace.

2 Villanelle for Century's End

Vera Moulton Green

If He calls me, what shall I say?
How in the turmoil play my part?
There's something waiting for me today.

Rushing around in sport or play,
Making a noise or being smart—
If He calls me, what shall I say?

Something within me prompts delay.
In a week, a month, a year, I'll start.
There's something waiting for me today.

The future offers a great array:
How can I choose? I need a chart.
If He calls me, what shall I say?

Teach? or foster? or dig? or pray?
Count the cost, or follow my heart?
There's something waiting for me today.

Shall I go forward or shall I stay?
Go with the gang or stand apart?
If He calls me, what shall I say?
There's something waiting for me today.

3 Hint from a Snail

Moira P. Pye

When foot
falls short
of spoken
thought,
do not,
for charity,
cry
"Pharisee!"

Thought,
leading foot,
finds star
and then
the
slow
foot
    comes
       where
          longings
are.

God shines on thought
that foot
may know
the way
to go.

4 End of the Comedy

Richard Howard

I've eaten husks, haven't you?
And was hungry on more than one occasion.

Leaving home (or so I thought!),
Running far afield and dancing,
Singing, shouting, laughing,
With perhaps just a little too much enthusiasm,
A little too much energy.

Voice screeching
Heart reaching
Thoughts turning
Soul yearning.

Ah, the patience of my friends!

Joanne said, "It's the search for God."
I looked at her.
"I recognize the symptoms," she said,
"I've eaten the husks." Silence.
"The husk-eating pit isn't bottomless.
You come to the end soon enough.
The end of the husks. The finish.
Finita la commedia."

And I did. I came to the end.
Being left out, I turned in
And found God.
Found Life. Found Love.
Found not husks, but sweetness of honey . . .
Wine of inspiration . . .
The firmness of the Rock . . .
The innocence of the sheep . . .
The healing of the leaves.
Found my Father's mansion.

5 Remembering the Dove

Pearl Strachan Hurd

Restless within the ark,
shelter divinely provided,
I longed for wider space,
but the waters had not subsided;
the struggle with self went on,
though the rain had stopped, and above
the sun already shone.
The rainbow was still to come.

And then I remembered the dove,
the small bird sent to explore,
released by protecting love.
And the dove, having found no floor
to set her feet on, returned
into the shelter, and waited.

A second time she flew
to reconnoiter before
obedient Noah moved.
Olive leaf had to show
flood gone from the land,
soil ready again
to support, to leaf, to flower,
to nourish, to bring to fruit.

Love knows when to give
the signal; knows when ground
is solid beneath our feet:
knows when we must go forth
and replenish the waiting earth.

6 The Appointed

Doris Peel

Those with young,
   those with a vision faithfully held
       as the child is held to its destined hour

they will be led
   through every trial, from the cruelest heat
       to the bitterest cold. They will be steadied

when the harsh winds blow
   and, in a deadening drift of mists,
       be summoned to proceed by a way unknown

as over and over they are told:
   It is I who have called you to this role.
       I who have caused your steps to turn

from the small hearth
   in the sheltering room—out on to this
       rough mountain track that only can lead

to the heights ahead.
   O Mine the command that works in you!
       from the vision sown to the bringing forth

not on some far
    unsullied star, or eons beyond
        all claims of now—but here, right here

in space and time—
    of what from the outset I have known
        as *your* task. In My design.

7 Ballade for the Commandments

Neil Millar

They stand, but not because, of old,
    A prophet tuned his inner hearing
Into eternity, and heard. They hold
    Steady against the windy veering
    Of ancient sin and modern sneering—
The golden calf, the yellow press—
    Simply because, diverse, cohering,
They are the rules of happiness.

This way to joy. No harsh and cold
    Half-human god, no domineering
Heavenly tyrant sternly doled
    Dangerous don'ts to us. No searing
    Lightnings attend our Father's rearing.
The Ten Commandments speak to bless,
    And echo in a storm of cheering—
They are the rules of happiness.

When tiny weeping Moses lolled
     Cradled on water, loudly fearing,
And Pharaoh's daughter, brown and gold,
     Stood puzzled, delicately peering,
     Her gods inert—her Spirit, steering,
Guided her fumbling first caress;
     The Ten breathed through the reedy clearing;
They are the rules of happiness.

Older than Egypt, still appearing
     Newer than fashion's latest dress,
Still urgent, relevant, endearing—
     They are the rules of happiness.

8 Israel Thinks of Esau: Evening

Paul Osborne Williams

After all my flight, my years away,
He thinks no ill of me. We both are blessed,
And not, as I once thought, by trickery,
But by the Lord alone. He gives and gives.
Laban surely taught me of disguise
In darkened tents. My own trick turned on me
Cost seven years of service at his hand,
As well as exile at my own. But now
I've learned so much about agreement with
The Truth, and Esau has his blessing, says,
"I have enough." Of course, I should have known
And not have feared this morning when he came—
My brother, now you're twin to Israel.

9 Ring and Robe

Rosemary Cobham

The ring and the robe
Are for all who are journeying homeward,
Much valued sons of God
In the joy and the light of returning.
Shoes for repentant feet,
Fatted calves for the feasting;
The swine and the husks recede;
Stilled is the yearning.

Love in the Father's eyes.
(*O brother, brother, love in your eyes also?*)
Those who were lost are found;
Those who were dead, live;
Those who were gone are returned
(Lessons learned, nothing left to forget, forgive).

Let music explode in the land!
Let everyone dance and sing!
For those—the redeemed—the robe;
For each loved son, the ring.

10 At This Very Hour, in This Very Place

Doris Peel

It must have been quite
a usual day
for everyone else
in that small town

when Mary—
marvelously spoken to
as no woman ever
on earth before—
tremblingly received
what would come to pass
for a world beyond any
world she knew.

It must have been quite
a usual day
when—later on—
from that same town

someone who faithfully
had waited there
until he was told
"Now begin—"
strode without any
fanfare at all
down from his hills
to Galilee's shore.

For isn't it *always*
a usual day
for those who haven't
(wherever they are)
so much as a clue
as to what goes on
in a nearby street
or even next door?
Who catch no call
unaccounted for;
no sudden flash
on the air; no hush
pervading again
as it did of old
some prophet's room
in a neighbor's house . . . .

So now as this Tuesday
or Thursday draws
(however unmiracled)
to its close

remember that
        nearer than dreamed
                        perhaps
an angel has called
on someone else.

"Stand still and they will gather."

Comfort

11 Doves

William B. Lynch

I want
the words to flutter
around you and land softly
on your shoulders in peace.
I want you to hear them
tell you of heaven.

Stand still
and they will gather.

12 Summoned by Psaltery, Timbrel, and Harp

Doris Peel

It is not said
    that mourning shall be turned into non-mourning:
    a cessation of suffering, a merciful blank
    like the aftermath of a crisis passed.

Nor is there promised
    the prolonged privileges of a convalescent
    who earns—by the mere feat of survival—the
    flowers, the fruit, the ministrations of others.

For behold
    it is dancing—
        dancing—we are called to!

O summoned we are
    (from the darkest depths)
        to that act of gladness

that elated leap
    even the new lamb, come to earth, straightway knows
    how to perform: bounding up on stiff little legs
    with no more reason for what it does

than the very joy,
    still fresh in it,
        of being—unhistoried—

what it is.

13 Today

Althea Brooks Hollenbeck

Today belongs to God.
Before it I stand
singing songs to God.
Whatever of bitter or sweet it may bring,
I will find its meat, and eat—
and sing!

Today is the table
God will prepare before me
with food He has blessed.
I would not dare find fault with the fare—
I am God's guest!

14 In Good Company

Sandra Luerssen Hoerner

You are part of a great company
of good men who have encountered crises.

Is despair your great flood?
God will provide an ark.

Is fear your den of lions?
God will shut their mouths.

Is disease a Goliath?
It shall utterly fall because of
one small smooth stone of Truth.

Is impasse your Red Sea?
God will open up a way.

Is pain a prison?
God will break all chains.

Is threat of death a tomb?
God will provide a resurrection.

Each cross will be crowned.
God's delivering angels are at work
in every age for every man.

15 Security

David Littlefield Horn

No danger lurks without
    When deep within
No fear is found
    Nor unrepented sin.

Each day I pray to love
    My neighbor more
And find one Mind
    On both sides of my door.

16 Lions and Angels

Margaret Tsuda

O king, live for ever.

The accepted salutation
of the day to a
mighty ruler
must have had
special meaning to
Daniel after a long
night spent with
the great beasts—
hungry,
whining, and snuffing
in frustration.

But, let us
remember, that
night was also
spent with angels
soothing both
man and beasts with
the consolations of a
mercy and of the
divine, preserving Love
which can deliver
from every fear,
fill every need, and
provide an angel
to companion
         any occasion.

17　The Divine Embrace

Exodus 20:4–6

Carol Chapin Lindsey

"I . . . am a jealous God." Vindictiveness,
Like mist before the light, evaporates
As higher meaning floods the thought: "I claim
My own and hold them now, for they are Mine.
No lesser power can or ever will
Loosen My grasp upon My very own.
I will not lend them to another mind.
I cannot give them to another god.
As sunbeams are forever bound to sun,
As drops of water with the sea are one,
As flowers and fragrance cannot bloom apart,
So spring My own ideas: eternal, Mine,
Hid deep, kept surely, purely in My heart."

18 The Coming of the Christ

Iolani Ingalls

That night, sudden singing:
so that, tonight, in Cape Town and Atlanta
shepherds awake!
The wondrous laser beam,
for all its special properties,
piercing between molecules
has not that certain way with light
that can shine day
into a heart's or a world's night.

19 Garden Night

Stephen Gottschalk

Depth unto depth at that hour.
                    Outside the garden
the stars still whisper of cosmic things,
all unaware that they are being tossed
and juggled like toys.

                    The leaves rustle,
unsure of that final night's rumblings.
     See, he arises,
the angry hour upon him;
his will, quite dumb now, has sped
into the garden rocks, where it will
gather silence and be still.
     Strength is now the angel of his gloom.
                    Ah, see, he comes forth—
this is the first, the night's resurrection.
He comes forth,
     and, Lord, what sorrows are lifted at thy
                              rising!

20 Continuing Drama

Neil Millar

Death spares us not a challenge, gains release
From no reluctant duty, stern indenture;
There's neither flight nor conquest in decease;
To die is not "an awfully big adventure." [1]

Death has no terror, is not preordained:
It is a fraud, a specious counterfeit,
A play-within-a-play, and doubly feigned:
We do not see it through: we see through it.

Only an audience with dazzled eyes
Grieves when, on stage, a skillful actor "dies."
The curtain falls; the fallen actors rise.

Outside the darkened theater of sense,
In Life's perfection, Spirit's permanence,
There is no dying—even in pretense.

[1] *Peter Pan* by James M. Barrie.

21 Immutably Themselves

Doris Kerns Quinn

We know not yet what they shall be
When we shall see them as they are;
We'll keep the essence of them free
We will not think of them as far.

When we shall see them as they are
No longer hidden by a veil,
We will not think of them as far
We will not think of them as frail.

No longer hidden by a veil,
No longer vague, no longer dim,
We will not think of them as frail—
The bygone her, the former him.

No longer vague, no longer dim,
They are immutably themselves
(The bygone her, the former him,
Not memories laid away on shelves)

They are immutably themselves:
We knew them once, we know them still
(Not memories laid away on shelves).
Illumined by the Father's will,

We knew them once, we know them still.
How strange that we had thought them gone!
Illumined by the Father's will,
They shine as they are shone upon.

How strange that we had thought them gone;
We'll keep the essence of them free.
They shine as they are shone upon—
We know not yet what they shall be.

"I am His own, not wondering what I am . . ."

Individuality

22 Countdown to Sunrise

Rosemary Cobham

I lie here quietly (long before the sky lightens
And the dawn comes) establishing who I am—
Beloved child of loving Father-Mother,
Unpressured in the equipollence of Soul,
In true being perfect as the Father in heaven is perfect.

I am cradled in eternity. No mortal history
Past, or present, or threatening in the future
Can drag me down. I am no anxious swimmer
In river where waterweeds clutch. I stand on Horeb
In clean, pure air of everlasting Truth,
Innocent in unfolding sense of Being,
Loved and loving, knowing no coming or going,
Alone, but not lonely in the infinite family of Spirit,
Secure as bird in open firmament of heaven.

I am His own, not wondering what I am;
Contented to be the expression of His I AM;
And in the marvelously clear light of this awareness,
I lightly rise to explore eternal day.

23 Identity

Carol Chapin Lindsey

Cog
digit
number
speck?

Computers would take over
if they could
our very selves.
In the myriad externals of today
where are we?

Mind reckons from within.
Soul never loses sight
of its own forming.
The vast soundings of our God
will ever bring to light
each one an image of the All:

distinct
inviolate
individual
himself!

24　What Eye Beholds the Spring?

Joyce Grenfell

What eye beholds the spring?
No retina or lens
With signals to the brain
Could compass such a thing.

If on this earth we see
The green immensity
And hear the music's ring,
Where can the real spring be?

From time to time the mind
Sees more than mortal's range,
The universe made plain,
A seeing for the blind.

It is the eye of Mind
That sees and hears and knows
The law that holds intact
The man, the star, the rose.

25 The Microscope of Love

Margaret Tsuda

Snowflakes go
flurrying or blizzarding by—
a wet, misty blur.
On the ground
snow felts together
in a white wall-to-wall.

Or so we see!

But the microscope's
enlarging eye
rejects snow,
chooses snowflake,
astonishing us with
revelation of
intricate, crystalline patterns
infinitely varied,
each unlike all others.

Why cannot our eyes see that?

Peoples cover
continents of our planet.

Beyond the narrow
band of kith,
do we not see faces
in a featureless blur—
"the public," "the masses,"
"hard-core unemployed,"
"overprivileged,"
"victims of *x*,"
"inhabitants of Y"?

But the microscope of Love
denies demographs,
statistical tables,
lifts man
out of mankind,
focusing the
light of Truth
on each beloved son,
so that expression, form, and color
stand out in
perfect individuality.

And we too can see this!

26 And in Their Mouths Is Found No Guile

Doris Peel

They who stand with the Lamb on Mount Zion,
having the Father's name written in their foreheads,
sing a new song.
    Innocence is the theme of it—
innocence fresher than first-of-morning light,
sweeter than waters fountaining from a source
high in bright hills.

The sound that comes
    is frail as a flute, is pure
        as the shyest of woodland calls.
It is all child in a ruffian world.

      O how can it hold?
            How prevail?

No one can tell. No one knows

until—at last—
    returned to his own immaculate mount—
each finds issuing from his own throat
        the song that was his
before the world.

And so, as himself the singer, knows.
And so can tell.

27 The Shepherd Boy

Elizabeth Glass Barlow

He would not take the borrowed sword
Or put on armor not yet won;
Instead, he trusted well-tried truths
To prove that he was God's own son.
These woven fast into one whole
Sufficed to make his coat of mail—
A garment of omnipotence.
Clad with this, he could not fail.

O let me know myself to be
Clothed in robes of honesty.

I will not take the borrowed plume
To wear and wave it as my own
Or drop my faith in fear's abyss;
Unarmed, I stand with God alone,
My sling and stone Truth's power unleashed,
My speed the here of instant good.
The giant who comes facing me
Dissolves before Love understood.

O let *my* shepherding ever be
Unselfing self and finding Thee.

28 In Bethlehem

Adrienne Mead Tindall

No other way could tiny child have been protected quite so well.
    A world attuned through inspirationed prophecy
    to glorious marvels faithful ones would grasp.
    A gentle mother pure as love itself,
    her heart prepared to cherish her own babe.
    The kindly Joseph ready standing.
    Long a righteous law-led man, yet
    loath to even righteously condemn
    a sin that was in fact no sin at all.
    And when inspired insight guided sight,
    a shield from shaming sneers of "friends."
    Nor would decree-forced journeying
    make him desert his close-held guardianship.
    He took her with him as he crossed the land—
    to David's Bethlehem.

    The place of travail might have seemed untoward,
    but had it not a hallowed quiet?
No other way could secret sanctuary have been provided quite so well.
    Not hometown curiosity, mortal fears,
    or small-thought doubts.
    No tired rowdy travelers crowded in, nor
    years' accumulations of civilized decay.
    A fresh-filled manger with sweet-smelling hay
    was ready to receive the tiny one.
    The placid beasts that stood nearby
    could well support the heavenly purpose—
    steadfast in their warmth, content in
    only-natural-as-sunrise birthing.

No other way could heavens proclaim the grand occurrence quite so well.
A worldwide astronomical phenomenon
startled awake the learned minds to what
was happening long desired. And with a
steady leading, guided the far-searching thought
to a child
Uniquely sheltered, unmistakable, recognized without delay.

In fields nearby were shepherds
free as God ordained His Abraham to be
of worldly burdensome encumbrances.
Their unentangled hearts heard angel voices!
Heard the radiant assurance of
God's shepherd-caring for His well-loved flock.
Nor was there any courtly pomp to stay
their faithful drawing near the heavenly child.

Within the reign of edgeless Love,
Whose all-embracing care is wisdom's charge,
is found Love's saving message for each yearning heart.
And Love provisioned well its holy messenger—
mightily and meekly witnessed,
secretly and sweetly cherished,
shielded, long awaited—loved!

With every need assuredly supplied, as could be done so well no other way.

29 Your Day, Brother

Godfrey John

In you, His kingdom. In you, friend,
    the realm in which His will is being
    fulfilled rhythmically   deathlessly   irrevocably.
    Your identity remains
    changelessly distinct and yet
    unfolds the infinite
    individuality you have.
    Like the sea . . .
    Forever each cresting wave
    is followed by its sisters—yet
    each wave in you breaking now
    is never like the last.
                              Your brightest hours
    are Spirit's baptismals that spill
    ceaselessly along time's shores.
    Your agelessness
    is underwritten by His hand
    which moves unheard between the stars.
    For all things bear His signature.

    This day is yours, I say.

To find God's day about you is to
    find His seventh day sanctified, to
    glide into the high noon of your being.
Lift up your hands, look up! What day is this?

    Son of God, this day is His—
    is your day, brother—is beautiful.

30 Participation

Doris Kerns Quinn

I was not a joiner—
something of a loner;
not organization-minded.

Oh, I loved the truth!
I loved the church triumphant.

But I thought I had the right
to work alone.
No, I was not a joiner—
unique, individual
(perhaps above it all?)

Then Truth thundered at me—
blazed away
until my ivory walls
grew smoky—lost
their lovely glow.

And I saw the people working
in their beloved church,
working side by side
bearing "the burden
and heat of the day"
while I in my safe
privacy and pride
stood all aloof.

Then not only my walls—
my ivory walls—
but also my protective roof
collapsed,

And I was ready—
ready to be a joiner,
to be steady
(a lively stone,
but steadfast)
no longer weighted
by a heavy sense of self,
a struggling mortal mind
encased in matter.

I glimpsed my true identity
timeless and unconfined.
Leaving my ruined tower,
I joined the body
of devoted workers—
and I was strengthened
from that hour.

Oh what a breaking down began—
of fear, of pride,
of selfishness, of sin!

How the world widened,
how the light poured in!

31 "A man's gift maketh room for him"

Proverbs 18:16

Maxine Le Pelley

The gift makes room!
No
pinching
poverty
of doubt
can starve
you
out
of your
large
upper place
in His
forever
sun.
Heavenly rights
secure
one.
Reflection's
artistry
will
trace
unshadowed
your
original grace.

So gently groom
and shape
to lift
what must
be known
first as
His gift
to be
your own.

32 Christmas Gift

Max Dunaway

Here is a Christmas gift, O God,
For You and Your dear Son.
It is my life: may it show forth
What Your great gift has done.

33 After All . . .

Joanne Mazna Garinger

After all those wretched
no-answer type prayers
of endless asking (be honest, self,
it almost came to begging, didn't it?)
   yes but
after all that terrible wanting so badly
to see the truth/the good in me
   so much
so laser-like the light that broke
so clear so clean too long delayed
(that dawn-coming oncoming I)
that I leaped from bed pure laughter-full
   so *seeing*
saying
Father, what a wonderful Mother You are
what an infinite sound Your verb to be
   and singing
God, what an amazing ascending
idea You had
when You had me

"From whatever step on the upward stair..."

Aspiration

34 Truth's Spiral

Phyllis H. Stoddard

From whatever step
on the upward stair
I reach for His hand
I find Him there.
He does not know
my dreams of start and stop;
this spiral has no bottom
and no top.
The steps behind, below,
dissolve away—
I learn in Soul's undimming day.
Each successive upward step
by God is wrought
on these, my steps of thought.

35 Prayer to God

Anita H. Rosenau

Prayer to God
is a forward journey,
a grasp of the infinite,
an encounter with eternity.

36 Expecting You

Christine Estes

Expecting You is nourishing
as the promise of sunrise—
the one I've hungered at 5:30 a.m. for,
hurried for, frozen for,
and finally hung there, breathless.

Your coming is like that.
Immediate and colorful.
The largess of Your presence, Father,
reaching its accurate blessings
quickly and bountifully
into my huddling soul.

Worth braving that first hidden hour
tight with anticipation,
for beyond this particular coming
I treasure a tumble of arrivals.

So I wait, most patiently, with my colorless hunger—
because You are coming,
have come, will continue to come,
and have always been here.

37 Walk with God

Genesis 5:24

Gerald Stanwell

Have we sensed
the challenges he faced—brave Enoch,
when the world, youthy and green, had scent
of valleys, saw the distant hills
transmuted into gold-leaf splendor, tracing
the rich variety of life?
Enoch viewed exciting glints of it.
We do not know
how much he shunned the clamor of a vain and
sensuous world. We are sure he loved Methuselah,
loved all his family well.

Perhaps he talked with God in solitude, came
"close" to Him
in everything he did.
Could this "coming close," this "walk," be halted or disturbed
within a fledgling world?
And did petal or unfolding flower speak
of Life's unending tenderness?
Enoch must have worked with good.
Was he "in step" with innocence of heart
in beast and bird and man—when God took him?

Was there any place
in all his thinking for any tinge of gloom
when this transition came?

Suddenly,
like music of a voice, rising note on note,
each surpassing the melody
before, with nothing lost of
all its beauty,
Enoch walked with God without
the flesh, but consummate, serene, exulting more
in Love's ascendancy
as triumph and the destiny of man.

38 On Hearing the Good News

Virginia Thesiger

O let my feet run
fast upon the mountain!
Let there be no delay now.
So sweet the Word on my tongue,
the truth at my side
like a delivering sword;
here in my heart, my thought,
the glorious message;
the cup of healing
filled to the full in my hand.

No doubts now.
Truth cannot be gainsaid,
Love ignored, Life denied;
there is no going back,
no argument.
Only the sureness
and the leaping desire
to run down the street that is Straight
to find my Saul.

Like Ananias
  hearing God's call, I cry
"Behold, I am here, Lord."
  Here with the thundering news,
  the marvelous joy,
  with the Word and the cup
  and the sword held high.
  O yes, yes, Lord, here am I!

39 Among Those Present

Doris Peel

And then there was that servant of the high priest
                    who was—remember?—
struck at, impetuously, by one of us. One of those, that is,
on the right side. And a brave man too, when the crunch came.
For surely he risked by such a blow
     on behalf of the friend he addressed as "Lord"
being then and there cut down himself.

                  He's plain enough!
(All through time!) The *good* one, with sword in hand. But that
other man, that random servant—suddenly caught up, by a fluke it seems,
in the whole vast drama about to begin—
     now there's a character with a question mark!
His right ear severed. Zip, like that. Then touched, and restored,
by the very fellow they had come to seize.

What in the world did he make of it?

                Perhaps not at once.
Not there, I mean, in the thick of a scene that must, after all,
have been none too easy to figure out:
     with its melee of elders and officers and scribes,
all converged, as we know, in the uncertain flare of lantern and torch,
with blades drawn, and staves in the air, and somebody kissing
somebody else, while the usual onlookers—bound, no doubt,
to have latched on fast to so promising a show—
     jostled, gaped, even jeered perhaps, except for those few

who (as they tumbled to what was up) in a sudden sweat
took to their heels. . . .

                                        No, not then!
in the shock of it. But afterwards, when he was alone again,
lying wherever he went to bed:
      What did he think? What did he make

                      of that touch, that act?
                              That irradiating mercy
brought—like the remission for all blind wrongs
                                    (O all that would ever
in the world ahead be done in the dark by righteous men)—

to bear upon *him:* the injured servant of another power.

                              And later on,
at the unexceptional end of it all, with the troublemaker hung
between a couple of thieves, and all that high-flown talk of his—
on hillside and shore—now thrown back mockingly by those who watched,

      did he, this Malchus, standing there
                      did he look up—*look up!*—

And suddenly, as if spoken to, touch his ear?

40 Marriage

Margaret Singleton Decker

Companion, met within the great adventure,
hold my hand in love that casts out fear.
Together may we not reveal perfection,
the flawless knowing of the always-near?
Salvation sought is solitary, granted,
and yet, though each one see the dawning day
through cloistered vision, still the Lord's beloved
are drawn together on the upward way.

41 Love

Margaret Tsuda

Love
is like
a game of catch—
the easy back-and-forth
of an unscored ball.
No points counted.
No cups/medals won.

Even God
who is wondrous Love, Himself
giver of all love,
receives our love in
praise/obedience/thanksgiving.

And every father/mother
catching ball from
small beloved child
knows this is
the only way child
can be free to
receive again.

Love returned with love
is quite enough
to keep the game going.

42 Inner City

Elizabeth Woolley

There is an inner city
coming;
I see its form
evolving and its purpose,
and it is to be called
man.

Citadel man.

It will be infinite
(but not a colossus—
a stance between construction
and confusion).
Man, identified as everyman
but Spirit-made, singularly
original, and loved;
(his color, radiance)
safe.

Imagine you and me
compassed about with only friendly force,

walls not barred and tight
but light, fingers of light, framing
with glow
the growing things we have,
uninterfered with.

The inner city springing up—the city
has its rhythm/sound, the varied
tempo, singing, synchronizing
giving and receiving:
survival not an issue.
Just living.

The form is man-strength,
woman-loved,
portraying
the vision of Mind's creation.

Now we bravely, openly, tenderly, reflectively
dare to be the spiritual revelation,
that inner city.

43 This Moment of Your Living

Godfrey John

You're alive—not merely existing. You *are:* you're not trying to be. Discover the life of the moment—this moment of your living.

NOT YOU

Not you—as an amalgam of happenings, you-as-you-were a decade, a moment, ago: to ask What was I? is to be blind to the fact of presence. Man is not a chronology. Not you as a mosaic of hopes and fears: to ask What will I be? is to stop discovering. Not you content with a status quo: a cup of years spilling satisfaction over the hour. Not even you-as-you-becoming—

BUT YOU BEING

You spiritually. You in the action of being you where being is the emanation of I AM. "I AM hath sent me unto you": Being, God, impels man, breathes through him Love's incentives. Soul's expression now, you go as His fragrance in every place.

This is your felt unity with Him. Moment by moment.

Soul plants pure desires along your days. The innocence of what you are flares through the guilt of what you are not. Like cyclamen in the winter sun: not withholding, not seeking to hold—but giving out help simply by being what it is—moment by moment.

You Timelessly

Not you in the moment. But this moment of you—brilliantly,
immaculately. Knowing is being. Infinitely. Mind's allness, Mind's
oneness never stops being known. As man-idea, woman-idea—one
idea—in God's thought, you are instantly understood, always being
known; you have Soul's mobility within this hourless knowing:
the dance fulfilling the dancer without end, as beauty in the unspoken,
as rhythm in what is still.

Discovering

To ask Who am I? is to be irrelevant. To ask What am I? is to
be blind to substance, to the *isness* of Spirit where you are.

Ask, How am I being?

Man is what he's being—Love's pure idea—birthlessly real.

Love's meaning is your meaning at each moment of new awakening—
at the precision-timing of Principle. Here you are learning to be   what
you are. Beautifully. Brilliantly. Preciously. Agelessly. Mightily.
Deathlessly. Yes, as a psalm spills over you. Yes, in this fond discovering
of you. You are what you are because I AM THAT I AM. Now.

Moment by moment by moment   by moment

"... the right to vision clearing."

A Wider View

44 The Right to Sight

Doris Kerns Quinn

Sight
is active use
of light,
the bright
appearing

right
in perfect focus
sight
is Spirit's might—
not matter's peering.

Height
nor depth
nor night
nor mortal
fearing

can hide
from us
the right
to vision
clearing.

45 More Blessed

Geoffrey J. Barratt

More blessed he
    than flesh-oriented Thomas,
who, leaning *not* on the senses'
    reassurance and fingered proof,
believes.

46 Idolatry

Maurice Jay

Some
who would walk on the water
must have a boat deck intervene.
Some who would transcend time
feel dependent on scrapbooks
and clocks (or fantastic
imagined machines), not knowing that Jesus
talked with Moses
through the effortless, natural inclusiveness
of elevated thought.
        Some, unaware
of their own deep desire to be buoyed
by boundless bright oceans of affluence,
are concerned
        about next month's bills.
Afraid to abandon a limited means
they begin to lose touch
with man's glorious end, and would then
sigh out their muddled and spiritless praise
to something so much less
        than God.

47 Multitude-loving

Patricia R. Allen

Although local planners failed to put a line in the municipal budget for
　　"multitudes, feeding of,"
Jesus and a quite ordinary Hollywood Bowl-sized crowd
　　from the neighborhood
saw Mind take form in substance, humanly perceived
that cool evening in a desert place.

"I have compassion on the multitude . . . ."
An all-inclusive Love, reflected truly by a single man,
　　fed the five thousand.

Things haven't changed much in two thousand years:
the ratio of prophets to the general population is about the same;
the hunger is just as great;
the Mind-source is just as near.

Continuing, I ask
who is my multitude—and where?
Simply those I encounter:
a subway carful, classmates, a church congregation,
fellow diners in a café, a grocery check-out line,
those around me on a beach, my landlady's family.
Media multitudes brought near:
the war-torn in Lebanon, Rhodesia, Ireland;
the unemployed and starving, the hostages and refugees;

not faceless masses to be skimmed over, but
  each one special in name,
  each one needful of light,
  each one precious to Love,
                    and therefore to me.

It's time to expand the heart;
no small-scale stuff will do it these days.
The budget is finite. Prophets have work to do.
You are the light—of the world.

So, Father, let me be Christly, radiant, discerning in response;
freely living that understanding of Love
which, infinite, has been ever enough,
even for multitudes.

48 Forever Active

Peter J. Henniker-Heaton

Man lives forever active at high noon.
He has no twilight years, no long declining
Toward an horizon that will hide him soon,
No cutoff date for retirement or resigning.

His life is not prescribed by solar orbit,
By phase of moon or stars that rise and set.
Dust neither made it, nor can reabsorb it;
No count of years can snare it in their net.

He has no wasting talents, powers decaying,
No faculties nor functions wearing out,
Rebellious organs, muscles disobeying—
God's law supreme within him and without.

The mortal sense of life drifts past below him,
As clouds that pass yet never touch the sun.
God is eternal Life; and as we know Him,
Our life is perfect, whole, with Him at one.

49 Matter of Fact

II Kings 6:5–7

Margaret Singleton Decker

"The iron did swim"
its weight as wood
caused by Him
whose law of good,
applied by man,
bids matter act
subservient
to Spirit's fact.

50 Exchange

Peter Allen Nowell

I love expanse of sea
and star-crowned nights
for blackboard thoughts
    (uncluttered
      simple
        free).

I love them as I love
    the shell
      the spider's web
      the leaf.
Exchanging these for thoughts—
what noble thoughts they are—
    those graceful curves
      and wonders of geometry
      in gossamer
        and humble symmetry!

For what will we exchange the sky,
for what exchange the sea?

For what but Spirit's vantage point?
Behold! Infinity. ! . ! .

51 No Barriers Here

Carol Chapin Lindsey

There are those who calculate
that when we rocket out beyond the moon
we come back younger
than if we had not blasted off.

Can't we then
begin to see
earth's scenes as passing shows
and let thought reach
the here-and-now of Soul,
a journey that outdistances
all downward pull
and bounds ahead
of farthest light-years
finally to find
Spirit's matterless space
where we really live and move
held forever
in the timeless caring presence
of Love's place?

52 Pure Mind

Peter J. Henniker-Heaton

God is pure Mind; He does not work through matter.
Mind needs no outside medium to express
its nature. All that Mind creates is wholly
of mental and spiritual substance, nothing less.

Man is pure Mind's idea. Not made from matter,
man needs no physical basis to sustain
his individual life. Mind's man and woman
pure thought in Mind eternally remain.

The pure ideas of Mind are not polluted,
infected, poisoned, pressured, fractured, strained
by matter. Their only atmosphere is boundless
intelligence, self-renewed and self-contained.

Pure Mind, controlling all in ordered action,
governs alike the atom and the star.
Wherever thought consents and hearts are willing,
its instant healings and adjustings are.

Mind has no place for matter in its eternal
purpose. But wholly spiritual, wholly good,
pure Mind's ideas, coperfect with their Maker,
unfold within pure Mind's infinitude.

53 Shoreless, Free

Maxine Le Pelley

Look from the sea
    Redundant sea
From ebbing, flowing
    Mortality's me.
Turn from the mist
    Of genesis—
Unstable Eden—
    Antithesis
    Of Love.
Think through
    To Soul,
Everness knowing
    No coming, going—
    And man,
    Love's image,
Shoreless, free!

54 Zion-prayer*

Patricia R. Allen

Arab, Jew—
Who are you?

Inspiration
    gives us grace
to see, beyond
    mere human face,

Man innocent
    in Soul's embrace:
minus matter,
    minus race.
Unrepressed,
    his dignity;
perfect, his
    integrity;

Uncensored and
    beloved his name.
God's universe
    he calls his home:

Mind's kingdom—clear
　　　infinity—
without disputed
　　　boundary,

Where no accuser
　　　trumpets wrong,
but angels sing
　　　a peaceful song.

Let every eye
　　　discriminate;
accept the real,
　　　abandon hate.

Let God's true love
　　　define all men
at one with Him
　　　and uncondemned.

* "ZION. . . . inspiration; spiritual strength" (*Science
　and Health* by Mrs. Eddy, p. 599).

55 "Rabbi . . .where dwellest thou?"

John 1:38

Pearl Strachan Hurd

At home he was and ready
on lake shore, in city,
to receive, to nourish,
to heal, to inspire.

They came, sometimes alone,
even at night, like Nicodemus;
sometimes increasing
to a multitude.
One of them had to climb a tree
to see, to be seen and recognized.

Few doorstones, hearth fires
for background of welcome
or personal invitation
or appointed hour.

Always at home and ready
stood that compassionate host
unwalled, unroofed,

to receive the desperate, the needy,
who came in and went out.
How could they question,
how doubt
their status as guests
in the Father's house?

56 When I Awoke in the Morning

Virginia Thesiger

When I awoke in the morning
and thought of the hours ahead—
the deeds to be done, decisions taken,
the tumble of words to be said—
when I thought of my long day's
journey into night (to filch a phrase)
I arranged to be terribly tired
by the evening.
And I was.

When I awoke in the morning
and thought of the hours ahead
with God at my side like a shining shield,
with joy running close before me
and peace bringing up the rear
and love encircling me round about
and blessings pouring, pouring . . . .

In fact, when I pondered
the light of the Lord guiding me through
the north, south, east, and west of my days
(to echo a phrase)
I arranged to be blithe as a lark,
fresh as a daisy,
bright as a button,
new as the morning
by the evening.
And I was.

57 Design

Frances Motley Pray

No measures based on mortal laws,
    No marring discords of decline,
Can alter symmetry of Truth
    Or shift God's beauty of design.

His rhythm moves beyond the scope
    Of lagging step or labored tread.
Its motion stems from hidden springs—
    Its source, immortal fountainhead.

And Spirit's melody transcends
    The muted tones of shadowed heart
Or stridency of disbelief
    By resonance of flawless art.

Inviolate, ordained by God,
    Life's music flows with perfect pace—
No jarring dissonance to mar
    Its harmony of inner grace.

58 Uncalendared

Peter J. Henniker-Heaton

Man has no hour of birth, no natal moment
when stars inclement
can fasten upon him some dark implacable fate.
From before the world's foundation
he has held his station
in the presence of God—individual, whole, complete.

Man has no hour of death, no mortal minute
that stores within it
some physical program coded to drive him hence.
Idea in infinite Mind,
having neither beginning nor end,
man coexists with divine intelligence.

Man does not come nor go; but under Love's care and favor
he lives forever,
his spiritual substance eternal, unimpaired.
From horizon to horizon
each appearing in its season,
he walks in Spirit, unclocked, uncalendared.

"(Oh, but my heart
flies out of the dream like
a singing bird!) suddenly I am free."

Healing

59 The Healing

Virginia Thesiger

After so long, so long
in my tight prison,
with my familiar shackles
heavy on head and heart;
after so long, so long,
suddenly I see the bars
with the eyes God gave me,
touch the chains
with the hand God made me,
and suddenly, suddenly
(Oh, but my heart flies out of the dream
like a singing bird!)
suddenly I am free.

60 Testimony

Acts 3:1–8

Rushworth M. Kidder

They were good friends, the men who laid
me daily at the temple gate
called Beautiful to garner alms
from such as spared, among their psalms,
a passing nod and a coin.

Those other two who passed that day—
how could my good friends know what they
saw at a glance: that I, who came
out of my mother's womb a lame
and beggared wraith of a man

had never come from there at all?
Could my friends shear my past away,
who only knew what I (and they)
had long heard taught: a terrible
fierce God and a fleeting man?

Yet we all felt it—the unsurprise,
the calm tremendous love, the eyes
that gathered in such truth as I
had always known, inside, *must* be
but never had seen in a man.

There was no crash. He said, the same
as I say it to you (and with
such simple meaning!), "In the name
of Jesus Christ of Nazareth
rise up and walk." I'm that man

who walks now, leaping and praising the Love
that—of course—God always was. Could I
ever again sit down in fear
when with good friends I can stand and share
this freedom no coin can buy?

61 Before the Dawn

Lyle M. Crist

Before the dawn
the song began!
Before the sweep of light
—no matter if it was moments or more—
this backyard bird
sang, knowing;
his melody a harbinger.

And I thought how
often, only after rewards were given,
I have sung—
but how
faith is a song

before the dawn.

62 When Is Now

Rushworth M. Kidder

When "if God does" gives way to "since God is,"
and all the *maybe's* melt to *certainly;*
when *my* and *mine* yield cordially to *His,*
and "here's for you" submerges "what's for me?"—

when platitude (the aged counterfeit
of artistry) crumbles at sounds of *new,*
and childish tough-talk (blown-up opposite
of tenderness) bursts at the touch of *true*—

then shall (in other words) the Word appear
charged with a force so fresh no age can fear
its thrust, no youth resist its crisp compelling
(because, at last, it lasts beyond the telling);

and then shall *now,* cleaving the dumbstruck *when,*
weave in our tongue the words that heal all men.

63 Radical Steps

Matthew 14:23–32

Richard Howard

You can call him what you like—
impetuous, brash, outspoken—
but once he recognized the Christ
and heard that command,
he did what the others didn't—
he stepped out onto the water and walked!
He didn't wonder, he didn't worry, he didn't wait—
he didn't even look to see if the others were behind him—
he just climbed out and walked.

Oh, I know! I know what you want to say—
that on Peter's part the story is a failure
because he floundered—but, friend,
because he had his vision fastened on the Christ,
that Christ caught him—reached through shrieking wind
and waves to uplift him beyond sinking doubt
and floundering fear.
That Christly rebuke was not because he had dared
to trust, but because he had not trusted even more!
Oh no, my friend, that short trip was a triumph!

And now, sailor, what about us?
When the going gets rough,
and the waves pile up,
and the wind is contrary,
and the command is "Come!"

which shall we do—
remain troubled and huddled and crying out,
or take those radical steps?

64 Wilderness Experience

Jack Edward Foss

I find myself in a desert,
my thoughts elemental—cleansed
    as pure forms shaped by God's wind.
In this silence I have heard
    His voice and I have
forgotten loneliness. The colors
    of the desert reflect
my own discovered peace. I know
    that I shall be sustained
as I kneel to drink Love's outflowings
    like water and gather
the precious manna of this morning.

65 Dragons for Unreal

Lona Ingwerson

That serpent was so little,
so subtle, I hardly noticed it,
but now it's a virtual dragon!

So?

Dragons aren't real,
only easier to see than serpents,
easier to see through,
ready for destruction!
(Not my destruction—
                                      theirs!)

66 The Collectable and Uncollectables

Doris Lubin

I proudly put my record on the spindle of personal sense
    and turned up the volume.
"I was right and you were wrong," so went the lyrics
    of my favorite song.
"Someone was wrong and it wasn't me."
Oh, I listened to that record frequently.

Then I realized there was a flip side I hadn't heard before.
It was called "Now Who's in the Wrong?"
    and I didn't like its tone
But I got the message. It was quite clear.
Any wrong is mine if I've given it ear.
If somewhere there's a fool—if with that I can agree,
    then I've taken error in, and the foolish one is me.

I'm throwing out the old records
    and now have as my goal
Listening more intently to the harmonies of Soul.
Oh, I'm tempted to listen, but not for long
    to an old melody, an old self-righteous song.
But I'm building a new, a most priceless collection—
One God,
One good, guiding
Every selection.

67 Believe Me—It Wasn't Easy

Marcella Krisel

For far too long
I played host to a problem
That I thought was up to me to solve.
I wrestled with it daily—
Denouncing, entreating, resenting it.
Unfortunately, it thrived
On all this attention
And the free room and board.
Finally, at a particularly low point
Of human discouragement
I was spurred into immediate
Action of a different sort
By a flash of insight:

"I can of mine own self do nothing." [1]

In what seemed then
To be a fit of recklessness
(Almost irresponsibility)
I tossed that problem out,
Out—with all its trappings—
From under my protective shadow
Into the bright sunshine.
There the light of Truth and Love,
Unimpressed, serenely
Dissolved and displaced it
In a matter of moments.

[1] John 5:30.

68 Justice

Althea Brooks Hollenbeck

Did you cast the stone—
criticize one of God's own—
or were you hit?

It cannot matter.
No stone was thrown.
God, who sees all, sees no one
but His own beloved son—
sees no enemy make a throw—
sees no guiltless take a blow!

69 "In the beginning God ..."

Genesis 1:1

Rosemary Cobham

You said: "I don't see where one can begin
To sort the muddle that I've gotten in;
And how can I be sure beyond a doubt
That God is real enough to get me out?"

Start with the problem, and God seems afar,
As starless night must seem from light of star;
But start with God and bring Truth's light to bear
On problem—and behold it disappear!

70 Offering

Cynthia Häfeli-Wells

Here is my little thought:
my tiny contribution
to the world's recovery.
Here is my heart's small prayer,
launched like a paper ship
on a dark, uncomprehending sea.
Only You know, O Lord,
and only You, its weight
and size and flexibility—
my grain of sand,
the numbered hair,
the water's drop in ocean's certainty.

I dare not contemplate
its microscopic touch
on earth's immensity.
But here it is—
I can no more hold it back
than cease to breathe—
the sweet insistent claim
that good must win.

For good was first
and needs not to begin.
It's now, and here, and there,
in blessing constancy.

My pinprick prayer is power,
an element of Love's supremacy.
In faith I send it forth
and trust its worth
to Him who counts on me.

71 "But where are the nine?"

Luke 17:17

Rushworth M. Kidder

Picture them waking next morning,
skin clear as sunlight, to realize:
"We never once bothered to thank him!

"Transfixed by the change in our bodies,
we never saw through to its meaning;
now we're fixed in ingratitude's history"—

The bitter remorse of the nine.

I've been there myself, have awakened
too late to the pith of a healing—
possessed of thoughtless indifference,

not grateful enough by a tenth.
Such a small portion!—this tithing
of all I've received of Christ's bounty,

this pause to give praise to the One.

72 Speak with Centurion Authority!

Luke 7:8

Geoffrey J. Barratt

Centurion knew
military command,
subordinate response,
one.

"Go!" he said.
 Gone.
"Come!"
 Came.
"Do this!"
 Done.

Knew too
Jesus' command
(with divine authority)
surpassed delay,
denied defiance,
dissolved space.

Healing sure
as we too
need but the "word,"
centurionlike:
 "Go, gloom!
 Come, light!"

Index

8-543210 7-98
0987654321